The Troublesome Amputee

Also by John Edward Lawson

Novels
Last Burn in Hell (Picaresque Book 1)

Collections
Pocket Full of Loose Razorblades

Poetry
The Plague Factory
The Horrible
The Scars are Complimentary

As Editor
Tempting Disaster
Sick: An Anthology of Illness
Of Flesh and Hunger: Tales of the Ultimate Taboo

The Troublesome Amputee

John Edward Lawson

With special thanks to Cameron, Philip, Dustin, David, Jeff, Jeremy, Linda, and Mike.

The Troublesome Amputee Copyright © 2006
by John Edward Lawson
All rights reserved

Published by Raw Dog Screaming Press
Hyattsville, MD

First printing 2006

Cover image: M. Garrow Bourke
Interior collage art: M. Garrow Bourke
Book design: M. Garrow Bourke

Printed in the United States of America

ISBN 1-933293-15-2

Library of Congress Control Number: 2006904115

www.rawdogscreaming.com

Acknowledgments

"Audited" first published in *A Little Poetry*

"Dead Cat Returns" first published in *The Poet Cabal*

"Dermabrasion" first published in *Best of the Dream People Poets*

"The East Coast is a Horndog" first published in *Bust Down the Door and Eat All the Chickens*

"Mowing the Pawn" first published in *Bust Down the Door and Eat All the Chickens*

"Sunday Crimes" first published in *Best of the Dream People Poets*

"Webster's Infidelity" first published in *In Our Own Words Vol. 4*

"Will Work for Food" first published in *Blood Cookies*

Contents

An Introduction to *The Troublesome Amputee*
by Michael A. Arnzen 9

Part 1: Apotemnophilia

Where the Heart Isn't 15
A New Leaf 16
Full of Flava 17
A Cut Above 18
Infomercial 19
Three Spider Sisters 20
Tricks of the Trade 21
Casket Climber 22
A Living Nightmarionette 23
Closet 24
Free Range 25
The End of the Affair 26
harelip 27
InDenture Servitude 28
Who's Been Nice? 29
Past 30
Bledful 31
No Protection, or: Trojan Strikes Again 32

Visiting the AbortAretum 33

Part 2: Acrotomophilia

The Troublesome Amputee 39
Plunder Revisited 42
Demands of the Voluptuous Virginal Sacrifice 43
Jung's Diet 45
Werewolf Limerick #1 46
Werewolf Limerick #2 46
Angry Princess Limerick 47
...And then She Left With His Money 47
The East Coast is a Horndog 48
Ambush Makeover 49
Lovable Lambchop the Mutilator vs. Super Virgin
    Dragon Girls 50
Hairy Trigger 53
Will Work for Food 54
Marvels of Horror 56

Part 3: Disarticulation

Wilderness Dump 63
Dead Cat Returns 64

Sunday Crimes (with Jennifer C. Barnes) 65
Dermabrasion (with Jennifer C. Barnes) 66
Deeper Into Faith 67
Automated Vision 68
The Wizard of Id, Revisited 69
Audited 70
Fuck Staying Hungry 71
The Good Girls' Soliloquy 73
Wedding Night in the Flower Bed .74
Performance Etiquette 75
The Difficult Resolution 76
DesensitEyes 77
My Grain Siesta 78
From London to Wall Street 79
Allahpolooza 80
Journalism Neuveau 82
The Strongest One to the Wallace 83
Mowing the Pawn 84
Expedition to Have 85
Matinee Gallery 86
Webster's Infidelity 87
The Chain Letter 88
Grandfather's Death Mask 89
After 90
Survivor 91

An Introduction to The Troublesome Amputee
by Michael A. Arnzen

WELCOME TO ONE of the meatiest collections of grizzly, grotey, bizarro poetry you'll come across. In other words, "the good stuff." The stuff you like to read. The guilty pleasure stuff that's hard to come by. Not the stuff you used to read from your lovers or childhood heroes, or the stuff you were made to read by your teachers or parents. The stuff you genuinely like to spend time with, musing and mulling and mashing. The stuff that makes you guffaw with laughter and want to read out loud to other unsuspecting people. The stuff you think about long after you've been soiled and stained and damaged by it.

Maybe this is the first poetry book you've ever bought, simply because you are acquainted with the author, or perhaps you're a new fan who just witnessed an amazing poetry reading by John himself. Maybe you're a long-time reader of John Edward Lawson's intelligently abject writing. Heck, maybe you bought *The Troublesome Amputee* because you're a stump fetishist, looking for a phantom kick. No matter how little or how much you might think you know about John Edward Lawson's work, you're about to be surprised. Maybe even offended. But you'll like it. You'll flinch, but it'll be too late: he's already knocked you to the floor. You'll find yourself on the pavement, quivering. Dizzy with delirium. But left wanting more.

Effective poetry is effective poetry, and it doesn't matter if you put it in a genre, like "bizarro" or "horror" or "goth" or "avant pop" or "the grotesque"—it's just good stuff. And *The Troublesome Amputee* is scary good. If I had to use one word to describe it, the word would be "audacious." This book has guts, and it takes you to places you don't want to go, but you will. It's filled with morbid curiosity, but for all its horrifying thrills, it's tamped tight with a passion for the marginalized and a concern for those in pain.

There tend to be two kinds of poets who write audacious verse like this: the kind who evoke our fear, dread, and repulsion through provocative language that ambiguously makes us somehow just as attracted to those repulsive things as we are disgusted, and the kind of poets who seduce you with their musings only to shock you with a surprisingly taboo idea jumping out of the jack-in-the-box structure of their poetry, just when you least expected it. John Edward Lawson is talented because he has mastered the art of operating on both levels, and his poems hit you like a one-two punch from that springy jack, bearing brass knuckles on his tiny puppet hands, leering as he lunges right at your face.

The dominant motif in this book is amputation, and even if not all of the poems are about lopped limbs and phantom feet, nearly all of these poems beg the question of "what's missing?" or "what's lost?" or "what's absent?" Sometimes that absence is just a subtly unspoken motive. Sometimes it's the lack the fetishist feels in his heart. Sometimes it's the unseen mechanisms at work that ambulate a body or body part. And sometimes it's about hunger, that animal instinct to fill up the hole inside us all in order to keep the furnace fueled.

In other words, it's always about us.

There are a lot of winners in this book, and I could go on and on analyzing what they mean to me. But instead I'll just recommend one to start with, for those who might not yet be convinced about this book. If I had to pick a favorite it would be "Will Work for Food." Call me disturbed, but I loved this over-the-top poem. As a writer of horror fiction since the 80's, I'd consider myself thick-skinned, but this one effectively grossed me out. That takes skill. The sick imagery here is masterfully wrought and the premise is so far over the edge that you'll find yourself marveling over the author's visions. Any poem that audaciously starts off with a flotilla of "zombie tongues" swimming around in a toilet bowl—and that's just the beginning!— has gotta be good. If you can stomach the ideas, you'll go on to enjoy Lawson's play with language a great deal...but the language will trick you in the end and send you right back up to the top of the poem, hungry for more.

This is the greatest sign of good dark poetry: it's compulsively re-readable, no matter how "wrong" it might feel to be reading such things. Lucky for you, it's collected in this wonderful book, which—if you still have your arms on you when all is said and done—you'll want to page through, over and over again.

Clipped,
Michael A. Arnzen
Pittsburgh, PA
March 2006

Part One:
Apotemnophilia

"Apotemnophilia is defined as self-desired amputation driven by the patient's erotic fantasy of possessing an amputated limb and overachieving despite being handicapped. The desire of a patient with apotemnophilia for amputation is obsessive, and a history of repeated, unexplained injuries to the same segment of the body is common among these patients. Patients with apotemnophilia secretly harm themselves to necessitate amputation of an injured limb, which creates a diagnostic challenge for the health care provider because of the atypical presentation of self-inflicted medical morbidity caused by apotemnophilia."

—Abstract from "Apotemnophilia Masquerading as Medical Morbidity," J. Mike Bensler, MD, Douglas S. Paauw, MD, FACP

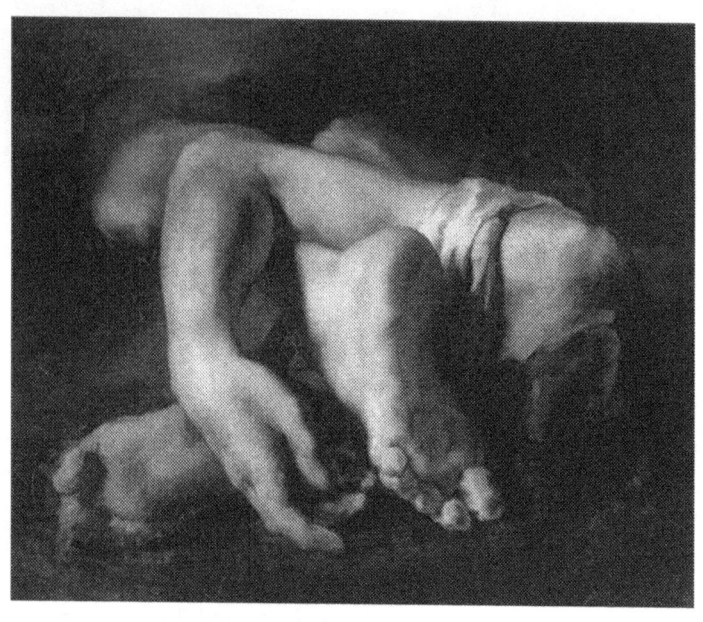

Théodore Géricault *Study of Truncated Limbs* about 1818-9

Where the Heart Isn't

I crept and slid among purpling children and blood
brambles in full bloom—I was afraid to breathe
Bullets hung in midair, the pollen of hate
seeding our streets, while your field lay blighted
In that field there was a solitary horse carcass
I nestled in its cartilage and glistening bone,
and when your screams reached my ears
I knew that I had finally come home

A New Leaf

Varicose vines spread
over skin, rupture ropes of meat,
take root in bone finding rich
soil in the marrow

The potter's field of your
body is lush now, green thumbs
in rictus arrangement, pruned away
for a perfect landscape of agony

Full of Flava

Kelloids: the Breakfast
of Chimpions has become
a favorite morning meal
among Caucasian consumers
aged 4-39, says a recent study.

Kelloids eaters regularly
watch *All My Chitterlins*,
both new episodes and reruns,
doing the Rerun Dance
while shouting "Dy-no-mite!"

79% of respondees own Eminem
albums, while 21% know African
Americans "on a casual basis."
85% believe "Black males can't
help killing people" and lock
their car door when they see
darkness moving on the sidewalk.

32% worry their significant
other fantasizes about Denzel
Washington, while 16% believe
that gorillas in the mist
really killed Jesus. 0% realize
Kelloids cereal is harvested
in the Inner City aggro-culture,
not in fields of agriculture.

A Cut Above

In childlike wonder
studying the scars
decorating the night
sky, with crimson
rain baptizing him,
he fondles his
razor necklace, tightens
it, and twists
just once, vaulting
one cut closer
to Heaven's shores.

Infomercial

Lose more weight!
screams the wild-eyed dietitian
Low-carb diet!
shrieks the audience
as the meat cleaver descends
Eat as much meat as you want
all while losing those love handles!
The volunteer, quivering, chews
a helping of raw meat, doing her best
to ignore the steady trickle
of blood down her hip and thigh

Three Spider Sisters

The three spider sisters
continually crawl over
each other, living within
a web of flesh—their own limbs
tangled and torsos colliding
and heads bobbing in time
with the audience's applause

Tricks of the Trade

The children stare wide-eyed at images
of cute puppy-wuppies and kitty-witties
lining his walls, while their parents are
more interested in the silent families
staring out from under framed glass.

"How do you get them to stay still,"
little Susie asks, pointing to the pets.
Mort chuckles. "Photographer's secret."

The brother and sister run all around Mort's studio,
knocking over a stool in the process.
"Hey," the father chastises, "You should be
more careful—anything falls on my kids
and I'll sue!" Mort nods, murmurs something
to pacify the indulgent parents,
steels himself for the session to follow.

The lighting is perfect, the backdrop is in place,
as is the plastic sheet over the carpet.
The taxidermy lessons are all paid for,
and now it is time to share his secret
for keeping squirmy-wormy children dead
still for the perfect family portrait.

Casket Climber

Her lack of energy
is conspicuous,
an accusatory finger:
she's one of *them*
A casket climber,
those family members who
just can't allow
their loved one
to take it lying down

They spot her too late—
already she has launched herself
onto the casket
like a drunken pelican perched
precariously on old pier pilings
squawking about her desire
to go with him,
and the flap she causes
overrides attempts to talk
her down safely

And the casket rests
agape, a darkened wooden oyster
already pregnant
with a formaldehyde pearl
But there's always room
for two, and the lid slams
shut, swallowing her
while the rest of the family
watches, stranded on decorous shores

A Living Nightmarionette

It dangles over the crib casting
shadows on the crying infant,
grows larger with each passing
night, feeding more aggressively
as proud parents smile at it
from the darkness

Closet

It is in the dark room
that his nightmares develop
Tiny fists pounding at
the door, fingers scratching
Musty clothes and mothballs
crowd in, press in suffocating

Unused tennis rackets are
underfoot with shoes that
kicked him, and boxes further
back hold black mysteries
from years gone past,
years in the light

Free Range

Claxon chirping sounds from blocks
away, reverberating from one high
rise carapace to the next,
a wordless song heralding the day's
catch—pink and soft-fleshed.
If not denuded mollusks, wonder
the gargantuan beasts, what are
these creatures of only four limbs?

The End of the Affair

Burnt sienna nipples flutter
under gossamer gown
like the batted lashes
of a coy girl in love

Burnt sienna nipples pulse
stirred to life
by the organ of desire
pounding within her ribcage

Burnt, seared nipples flutter
on the wind like spent ashes
desire scattered by wedding vows
exhaled so long ago

harelip

my ink gun kept
humming like applause
a thankful word arrest
caging their gloom
gravy rats talk
using word-ooze to
amputate your memory
tattooing thought terror
past the fat, the skin
striated muscles remember
convulsing hair follicles
my glue gun kept
interrupting your shrill
sentences—sorry
for being so rude
folks say my temper's
got a hair-trigger
now what did you
say about my lip?

InDenture Servitude

Your teeth blossomed
in fits of flesh lust
within my chest cavity
The growth spurts split
my ribs, replaced them
until my heart was ensconsed
in a cage of fangs

Who's Been Nice?

His short life was an uphill
race leading to this finish line:
paralyzed, as if his month-old
arms and legs could fight off
the knife, the clamps, as
if he could articulate the pleas
necessary to prevent his ribs
from being pried back, his organs
being dislodged and vivisected,
all while they kept him alive,
conscious, during the nine hours
that St. Nicholas was asleep.

A nurse ferried what was left
through the maze of incubators,
disappearing through the white
door in the rear of the nursery
to the hospital's waiting incinerator.

Past

He who is last does not always laugh
The exuberance of youth is growing cold
And this too shall pass

The tally of years is frozen, ice-cast
The realization of our child's mortality is one year old
He who is last does not always laugh

We tried to escape but got lost in each other's tracks
Fortified in our cage we believed we could be bold
And this too shall pass

The return to the crime scene was no easy task
You left early, I lingered with my heart on hold
He who is last does not always laugh

What you viewed as demure was the epitome of crass
Your "proper way" trapped me in its fold
And this too shall pass

All of our intentions became riddled by cracks
grown over with a five-o'clock shadow of mold
He who is last does not always laugh
And this too shall pass

Bledful

the crack in my head is opening
bloodless thoughts flood the darkness
reaching out now, hoping

bloodless thoughts flood your darkness
blackened beseeching breaching your safeguards
enticing, entwining, becoming your harness

reaching out now, hoping
the embrace you drape around my shoulders
is more than just tortured contorting

bloodless thoughts are my darkness
the crack in my head is opening
reaching out now, hoping

No Protection, or:
Trojan Strikes Again

boy, am i happy now
watched a woman being
tortured online and
depleted my bank account
and caught a virus
and can't find a cure
her baby was on a rocking
chair in the corner silent

credit cards and electronic
transfer of images and
sounds her mouth open wide
struggling to scream
distorted emotions fuzzy
and her friend set her up

my hard drive is melting
down and up into the wound
making my loins want
to cry with sound and
full motion streaming
over cheeks and screen

Visiting the AbortAretum

The revered art of bone-sai
is further proof of our technological
advancement, serving as recycling
and body art in one: the AbortAretum
takes one woman's trash and converts it
into everyone's treasure.

Visitors wonder if the air
conditioning needs to be
quite so forceful.

Glistening in glass cases,
on pediatricstools, dangling in midair,
dark sunspots enshrouded by translucent
eyelids stare at scholars,
wonder at elementary school
field trips they'll never take.

Teachers and chaperones try to suppress
the tremors in their voices, in their
limbs, for their own benefit more
than for the children. The young ones
do not connect this botany of flesh
with anything human, and in a way
they are correct.

The frigid air gusts stronger now.

Stop and listen to the bones sigh,
piping out ghastly burbles and
shimmering shrills blinding your ears,
draining the last reserves of courage

stored in your bladder.

In the cafeteria bored workers
dust the tables, wondering why
business is so slow. In the restrooms
condom machines overflow with money,
unable to meet the visitors'
ravenous demand.

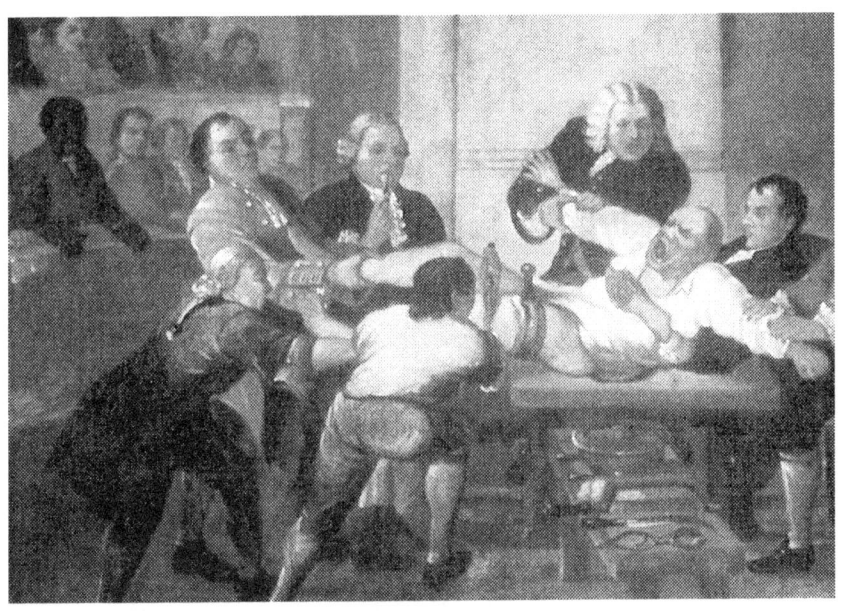
Picture of an amputation in the operating theatre of old Saint Thomas Hospital, London, around 1775

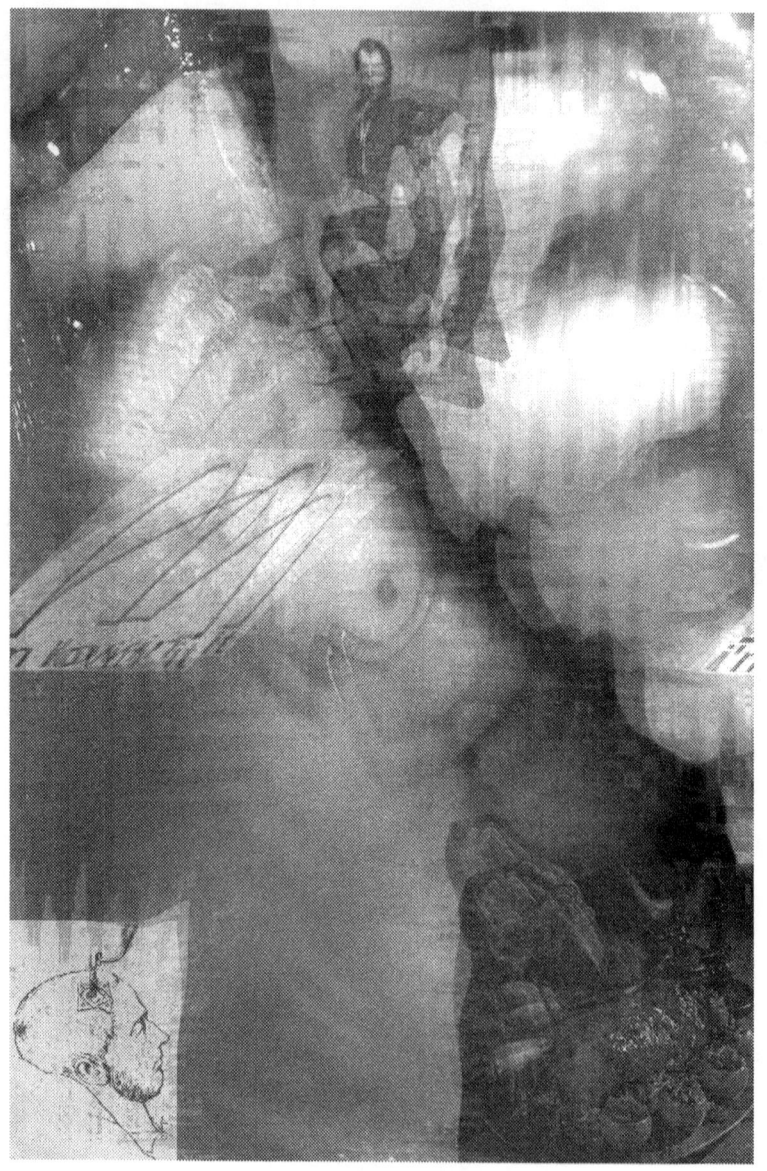

Part Two:
Acrotomophilia

"(From the Greek, akron, extremity + tomo, a cutting + philia—word ending meaning love, or erotic and sexual love of a person, thing, or activity)

Simply put, this is the medical term for the sexual desire of amputees. Someone who has acrotomophilia (in the clinical sense) is sexually attracted to persons with an amputation, and may be unattracted to people without amputations (although some can manage by fantasizing that their partner does have an amputation).

In its most extreme forms, a person my be unable to become aroused or achieve orgasm with anyone who does not have an amputation."

—*The BME Encyclopedia*

The Troublesome Amputee

The sky is a blistered
orange fist tightening over frail
office buildings and asphalt arteries
coated with plaque as George walks
to work, each step filled
with fresh hot coals and used condoms
seeding a thousand-mawed douche chill
in his gut—he knows what awaits him
not only at the office, but also
the thing lurking around the corner:
it is the troublesome amputee.

There amongst matted, urine-stained newspapers
nestles the squirming one, held
together by a decade of grime and grease,
by loathing and the expectorate of strangers.
In her excitement her truncated appendages
wag like the stump of a cocker's tail cropped
woefully short with those fucked up canine
nail clippers at birth, and she pants
laboriously while writhing in George's direction.

As always he attempts to scurry past
her thunder-imperfect pleas, all legless
threats armlessly embracing hope, and finally
she resorts to flinging her trunk
underfoot in an attempt at toppling him.
What does she hope to accomplish? Will she
snare his billfold between rotted gray tooth stumps?
No. She merely receives a kick to the cranium,
making this morning just like any other.

The troublesome amputee, not content
with merely scuffing George's shoes, latches on
using her moaning mush-hole and refuses
to let go. Perplexed by this development George looks
down at subhuman refuse in panhandler repose
with rictus smile wrapped around his ankle.
As most well-heeled gentlemen would do
he stomps. He half-runs, half-waddles in
the direction of his office/cell.
He sobs—to no avail.

A detail claws its way to the surface
of his murky red anger: the ends
of her stumps are crusted with barnacle-like
scabs that enable her to freak-slither
over the pavement as she does. Only,
on close examination they aren't scabs
at all. Collected and pressed into the abused
flesh of her limbs is post-consumer bubble gum,
scraped off the sidewalk, a psychedelic
pattern of armor and leggor hardened
by age, yet somehow still so tempting.

George wrests just one of the nuggets free.
The gray morsel holds no wisdom, no scrap
of paper with winning lottery numbers and poorly
translated Chinese sayings. The vacated space
it leaves in her flesh is pink-rimmed and
filling with flavor. The taste of malaise,
overcooked and left gummy on the tongue
like a night's worth of mouth-scum, oozes
purple-green and hideously sultry, turning
his argyle sock adornments into razor-toothed paisley.

These mutations dig into George's ankles
forcing a manic jig, an operatic tragedy

of decorum, carrying him away from the city's
arteries into its spurting wounds, areas
of truncated economy and cauterized hope.
The amputee stays with him, drifting on the eddies
of terror and insurgency leaking from her wound.
George's convulsive PCP boogaloo carries him
through one downsized thrombosis to another,
to another, each block more lightless than
the last. The feet at the ends of his legs are
unrecognizable to him, the scuffed shoes loaded
with creamy athlete's foot custard.

The amputee cackles in black and white,
snapping at his heels, and he knows
she is right. With feet like that
one must take a no tolerance stance.
Gleefully he chews through fabric, through
skin and fat, muscle and bone, splintering
his teeth. Rolling in the filth, eyes shiny
black oil slicks, a singular, elucidating agony
embeds itself at the base of his skull:
however devastating the situation seemed
from above, it really is much worse
now that he's down on the ground.

Plunder Revisited

Few people nowadays remember the Lusitania
was a pirate ship in its heyday, sewing wild
oates of "arr me hearties" and "avast ye!"

It sank in the shallows of Lake Eerie
and to this day the remains scream
ferrous oxide epithets, traumatized
by the Krauts' torpedo penetration,
its jeweled viscera splayed across the sediment

The crew remains on the bottom even now,
shaking phantasmal hook hands at jet skiers
racing overhead, gnashing teeth of ectoplasm
and roaring "Scurvy life-lubbers!"

Until the accident that leaves four
teenagers dead, young souls plunged
into the pirates' Grand Guginol Water Sports Club
damned to forever walk the plankton

Demands of the Voluptuous Virginal Sacrifice

Lucifer, I applaud your morals-shattering power
But if we're going to hook up,
let's do this right

I, the Virginal Sacrifice (hereafter
"THE SACRIFICE") do agree to be bound
by the following agreement:

The Sacrifice shall remain chaste
until a date mutually agreed upon,
and on said date shall die in ritual murder
(by means agreeable to Lucifer,
hereafter THE RECIPIENT)

Furthermore, The Sacrifice does affirm
that all her physical assets are natural,
and evidence to the contrary shall constitute
breech, rendering The Recipient's obligations
null and void

The Sacrifice, in return
for dominion over the 114th Duchy
of Hades—and majority share
in the fast food corporation of
The Recipient's choosing—
shall perform all household
and wifely duties deemed
reasonable, notwithstanding
torturing the damned

(grievances shall be mitigated by
a designated resident of Purgatory,
not by residents of either Heaven or Hades)

If your advisors find everything to be in order,
please sign, date, and remit ASAP,
so I can get fitted for a white gown,
and leathery wing accoutrements

Jung's Diet

They hooked up electrodes to her
ovaries in order to monitor the dreams
of human eggs. Most of them
involved an angry black skillet
while others were dominated
by hairy faces with lips stretched
wide, baring sharpened white
boulders. It wasn't too long
before the scientists decided
to detach those electrodes.

Werewolf Limerick #1

There once was a werewolf from Nantucket
who kept warm viscera in a bucket
    With sharpened talons and teeth
    he would rend human meat
to get at the marrow and suck it

Werewolf Limerick #2

Her husband was an uncouth beast
walking about on not two but four feets
    He could bat his eyes
    and tell little red lies
but her parents wouldn't come for a feast

The Angry Princess Limerick

There once was a ghost in a glass house
who wore no brassiere nor even a blouse
    Armed with huge boobs and a knife
      she made quite a sight
carving men down to the size of a mouse

...And Then She Left with His Money

In the salacious port city of Baltimore
a drunken poet searched for a whore
    He took her to a house called Usher
      Got tied up and cried "Baby, rougher!"
With a toss of raven-black hair she said, "Nevermore!"

The East Coast is a Horndog

Yes, it boasts a phallic Florida
and a Hotlanta spot to match. It's eager
to penetrate your Bay of Pigs. It dreams
of slipping in the back door of San Francisco,
even though that bay is a tighter fit.
The Golden Gate hymen would be ripped
asunder. Despite the fact that its Twin
Towers have been nullified, no longer capable
of being twisted and teased, it still
finds pleasure in the tiny aircraft swarming
like spermatozoa invading its hot, wet
swamplands. Oil pumps like catheter play,
garbage dump scat, ready to pounce "South
of the Border"—let the Prophylactic
Appropriation Committee note the need
for greater funding from the CDC.

Ambush Makeover

When we noticed him strolling down
the boulevard in Fallujah, we knew.
Those fatigues were just so tired,
those boots so brutish, the screams
so boorish. He was a fashion victim
if ever I laid hands on one.

First we altered his stride—a hammer
does wonders for disco-era macho strutting.
His hair was in desperate need
of some red; a wrench always does
the trick. The shave may have been
a little close, though…the texture
of striated muscle is Zen goth hip,
but if the razor strikes bone
you know you've gone a little too far.

Lovable Lamb Chop the Mutilator vs. Super Virgin Dragon Girls

Everything is peaceful and calm
at Super Virgin Dragon Girl High School—
even the bullies and nose-pickers
are staying out of trouble, when
who should loom huge and monstrous
on the blazing horizon? None other than
Lambchop! Oh, the fuzzy-wuzzy focus
of children's adoration for decades!
But why is Lambchop five-hundred-feet tall?
And why do her eyes glare
with such an ominous red glow?
If one were to ask, Lambchop
would tell them: "It's because I'm
a hermaphrodite! Now prepare
to die the horrible death
of a thousand marinades!" That is
Lambchop's finishing move, the gargantuan
coup-de-grace which has beheaded so many
during his/her power-drunk rampage.

Yes, a gender crises of bovine
proportions has been stewing
for decades, fueled by the fires of rage
slow-roasting in the pit of his/her
heart. But what can be done to assuage
Lambchop—who can stand against the fury
that has bloated like a Ball Park frank from hell?

Who? None other than the Super Virgin Dragon Girls!
Ultra Orange,

the fire-breathing hot-head with a heart of gold lamé!
Ultra Pinky,
keeper of the ten-acious talons of terror!
Ultra Greeny,
the rookie with the heart of a tiger—and hot pants made from its hide!
Ultra Red,
she's Freud's favorite and the scaly scion of skullduggery!
Ultra Purply,
the pernicious princess of pulse-pounding prose!
Ultra Sexy Superintendent
She ain't no virgin dragon girl—*va-va-voom!*—need we say more?
Confronted with this ferocious female
fisticuffin' force Lambchop's
mad mutton disease reaches a fever pitch.

Ultra Red sets to analyzing Lambchop's
dreadful actions, revealing the desperate
psychology behind his/her methodology.

Ultra Purply unleashes a very saddening
maddening kiss-off letter, so complex
that Lambchop would need to sit on the toilet
for a thousand years before figuring it out.

Ultra Sexy Superintendent bobs and
weaves in such a suggestive manner
that Lambchop's gender confusion becomes
gender perplexity, calling for an additional
two thousand years on the toilet at least.

Lambchop arrived with a beef but quickly
finds him/herself in quite a pickle.
Where can a suitable toilet
be found for the task? Whole towns
float away or are buried alive
in a poopy Pompeii whenever he/she

cuts loose. Fortunately Ultra Greeny
is taking a ceramics course and,
with the help of Pinky and Orange,
has constructed a steel-reinforced
commando comode, giving the LamCops
enough time to arrive on the scene
and slap the cuffs on this wayward
member of their flock.

Hairy Trigger

Maybe I'll go back to my room and masturbate
thinking about all the little girls I
could adopt and collect my soupy seed
in a vial and send it to that cute bank
teller with a love note reading: "I wanna
make a deposit, baby!" and they'll
spend hours sweating, wondering if that
white stuff is what they think is or if it's
some funky new kind of anthrax, or maybe
I'll just go back to my room and masturbate

Will Work for Food

Homeless zombie tongues lurk in toilets
shimmying around the loose stool of junkies
in a marinade of urine and blood
thicker than syrup, the undead tongues
slap against their porcelain aquariums
tap-tap-tapping out a message,
perhaps an S.O.S, before they find refuge
in the mouths and eye sockets and ear canals
of unwary cleaning crews
who scream when confronted with
the sensation of slick taste buds
slithering through sinuses, milking
mucous membranes, unleashing
unsavory undeadness within their throats
dragging the piss of syphilitic rectum wreckers
into stomachs and lungs, and still
the zombie tongues spread their unholy
condition, infecting their new hosts

The gore-splattered zombie cleaning
crews rise and scream, rise and lurch
in search of new homes for their hunger
rampaging into shopping malls
and concert halls, launching themselves
onto helpless flesh sacs, and the last
thing the gentrified bodies feel
before rotten teeth violate them
is septic breath moist with
anal mucous…and soon there are homeless
zombie tongues everywhere, purpling
erections jutting from mouths with
blood vessels bursting and tendons snapping

the tongues rocket forth and jab
into abdomens and thighs like
a horny dog with a wet beach towel
injecting torn sinews with contamination
insemination making something old
into something new, because anything
that moves will work for food

Marvels of Horror

The Human Torch

It seemed like a bright idea
at the time—the Olympics were
in a ratings slump, Death Row was
overcrowded, and all it took
was kerosene and a match to turn
the running of the torch into good TV

Mr. Fantastic

He's a genius with chiseled features
who does everything with perfection
But the masses don't want
to be saved from their impurities
—and they don't mind making a mess
when slaughtering their idols

The Invisible Woman

Whenever he strikes her
a patch of empty forms
instead of a bruise
and by their anniversary
there's no trace
of her to be found

The Thing

That gruff, rocky exterior
hides a soft side, a human
side being crushed by the avalanche
of his skintight superhumanity

Dr. Doom

Cursed by a name
passed along by his parents
he suffers emotional scarring,
tattooing a multifaceted map
of hate across his psyche
But the doctor's lifelong
struggles come to an end
with a simple name change,
deciding Dr. Joseph Doom
sounds much more inviting
than Dr. Gaylord Doom, Jr.

The Amazing Spider Man

So debonair when he swings
between apartment buildings
a red blur—Mary Jane's blood
dripping from his mandibles

The Mighty Thor

Always a troubled child
he sneaks away from dinner,
from his studies, from chores,
and peeks between clouds
to find ant-like victims
for his magnifying glass

Professor X

He orchestrates
their flesh-on-flesh,
their moans and screams
Externalizing the inner
conflict of his crippled
morals on film

The Red Skull

Every night is
All Hallows Eve: dripping wet
tricks for kids, treats for
his mirror, a crimson
mask of normalcy
in a world run
by madmen

Iron Fist

When his wife gave him lip instead of head
his hand froze fingers curled shut cold
and he thought it a gift weapon wielded
against her warm giving opened red revealed

When his daughters embarrassed him in public
his tongue went rigid dead with rivit-buds,
lips fused soldered trapped syllables of hate,
and the girls thought it a gift weapon nullified

When he ordered the deaths of thousands
his heart went sleek stainless hammered out
and the world community was shocked awed disturbed
by the thought he had a heart to begin with

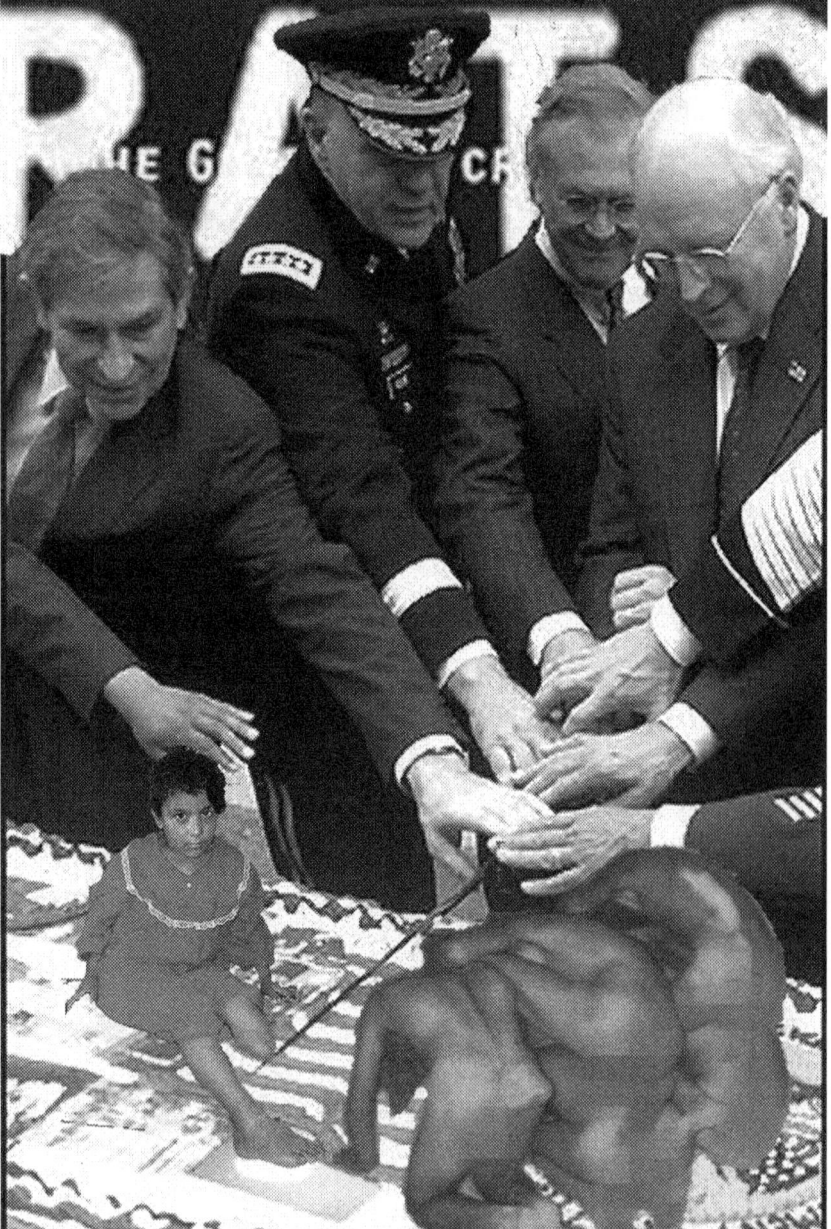

Part Three: Disarticulation

"Dis·ar·tic·u·la·tion (dsär-tky-lshn) *n.* The amputation of a limb through a joint, without the cutting of bone. Also called exarticulation."

—*The American Heritage Stedman's Medical Dictionary, 2nd Edition*

"The knee disarticulation results in an excellent weight-bearing stump. It is most often used in children and young adults, but is nearly always avoided in the elderly...Several advantages of the knee disarticulation include: 1) a large end surface covered by skin and soft tissues that is naturally suited for weight bearing; 2) a long lever arm controlled by strong muscles; 3) increased stability of the patient's prosthesis. A main disadvantage of the knee disarticulation is cosmetic."

—Amilcare Gentili, M.D., Musculoskeletal Section, UCSD Department of Radiology

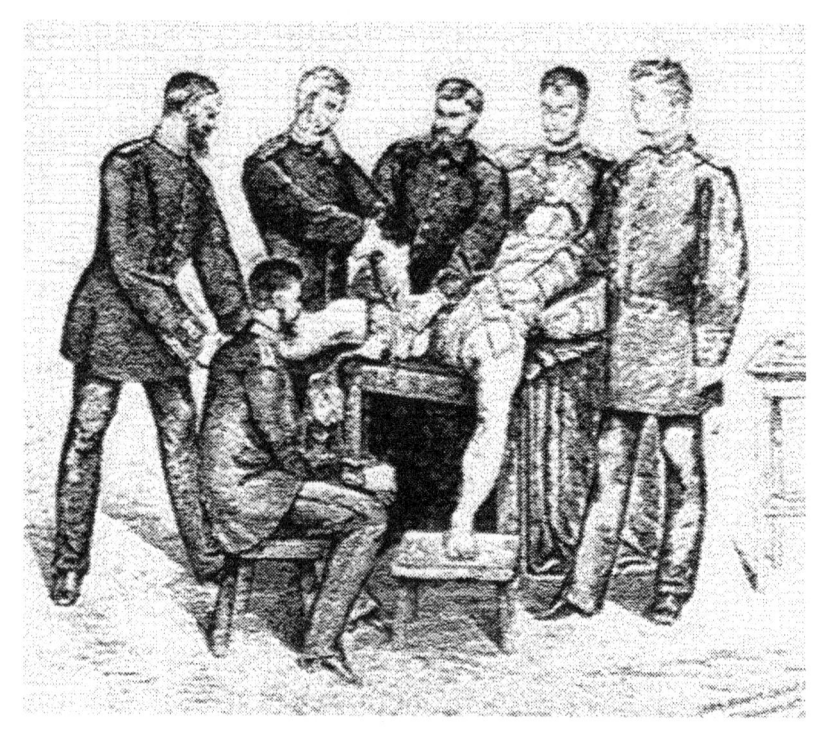

A Civil War Field Amputation circa 1863

Wilderness Dump

Life is
not at all
like a box
of chocolates,
but is instead
a confection coffin
of petite sores
with creamy pus-
filled centers, and
we are coerced
to keep eating
in the hope
that finding one
sweet morsel
will make it all
worthwhile, but
each is always
more bitter
than the last

Dead Cat Returns

Dead Cat dribble like Satan's basketball,
punctured, leaking hiss of secret syllables.
We only hum dead air, the cloying care
living have for the departed. Keep rolling—your irreverence
trails like incense, leading sonnet sharks to the remains
of your grammatical shipwreck. Flow like lyrical blood
in water and we'll seep into your home, flop in
your litter box of language. Jump high as you like.
We'll polecat vault, leaping over your distaste
in a single bound. Everybody bounce! Bounce! Yes,
we assimilate your give, your lightness of being, until
the gravity of our desire drags you screeching back
down to us…flat-Earthed fleas with feathered
quills to dip in your sacrosanct blood.

Sunday Crimes
with Jennifer C. Barnes

The gilt edge is invariably sharper than the torn
The blunt disguise of innocence eyed
warily from a distance through thorn-lashed lids
producing the prism of blood-lace vision
tatted with every shade of red

Unscrupulous lines cross-hatched and gartered
concoct an alphabet, describe a murder
of circles, a collection of crows
flapping their frenzy into hazy logic
unencumbered by pedestrian pangs
lavished on demure tantrums of fettered morality

Undeniably they stand for something
salute an ideal or copy-write a wrinkle
smothering imperfections into an obedient mask
another smudgy newsprint visage
wounded by an avid coupon collector

Dermabrasion
with Jennifer C. Barnes

The crack vascillates with time
unable to choose between a fissure's life of excess
and the wholesome thrift of homogeneity
sparkling with the luster of the anonymous
thoughts of contemptable crevices
the gritty grain of open space
jutting into oblivious mica and prosaic quartz

Defiant ruby blossoms grace the wound
incite the wind to whistle
at erosion's decorative textures
singing the ex-foliate's song

Deeper Into Faith

dancing maligned scars comprehend distortion
smiles echo water legs crossed gloves white
listen to the cameras blue and wet choking
a perception of filth innocent and you

Automated Vision

He believed in something he liked
to call kinetic poetry: the art
of rendering lyrical beauty in the flesh
The muse, to his mind, was
little more than a referee
in the full contact arena of life;
long, sharp nights became sonnets
while every day provided
a fistful of manifestos.

The Wizard of Id, Revisited

The acolytes gather in my receptors
chanting, beating drums, supplicating
to every sordid desire lurching in the
darkness between synapses, the poisoned
black mire of shifting tides
polluted with bodies I have known
I have seen, have conjured on my
invisible palate, painted white
with my crooked divining rod

It takes unrestrained ego to seek escape
from this outburst of sexual occultism,
yet no matter where I turn, my body
knows only one series of steps to follow
There are far more than a dozen of them
leading to Mistress Endorphin—can you hear
that sound? It's not a question of whether
her whip is cracking, or my spine, for they
are one and the same, and every time
the vertebrae tug at my skin those
ravenous worshipers speak in tongues
licking at my inner ears
until reason is silenced

Audited

Stayed up late in the confessional
again. Waiting for stale lies,
secrets dampening breath like whiskey,
and the stench of truth
burning as carelessly as discarded incense.

Can our sins be itemized,
catalogued and indexed in the hopes
of some existential rebate?
Clerical accountants insist on knowing
(between yawns).

Fuck Staying Hungry

When you get hungry enough to eat
saltines and soy sauce, come back
and we'll talk. When you get
hungry enough to eat grape jelly packets,
come back and we'll talk. When you
get hungry enough to scrape
bubble gum off the sidewalk and chew
it, then come back. And maybe
we'll talk.

When you get hungry enough to devour
your first born like it was
the last of a 41-course hunger strike
like it was that dollar-green rabbit
we hound around the muddy racetrack
like it was the carcinoma lingering
in your lover's heart, when you
unhinge your jaws and swallow it all whole,
we could talk then except you always
speak with your mouth full.

I have something to admit. I masticate
at least 12 times a day. It's out
of control. It's not even about pleasure
anymore, not when you do it this much.
The pleasure becomes inverted, the act
veering off course into the chasm
of masochism. I even masticate in public
—pardon me sir, may I borrow that hot
dog? Evening ma'am, might I partake
of your cream pie? Hey little kid...
how about a lollipop?

I've been charged with disturbing
the grease, inciting a diet, a salt and
peppery, exposure on flame grills,
it goes on and on. They remanded me
to the custody of Hungry Bastards Anonymous
and true to their name the members tore
into me, my body becoming a thousand
mouthfuls of greed, only to be defecated
in the communal slop bucket, because hey:
the scatological need to eat, too.

The Good Girls' Soliloquy

Laughter or screams echo shrill
From this distance we can ignore it all
but for good girls there is no
horizon, no wide open sky
Life is defined by a box
of innuendo, of possible reproval

Wedding Night in the Flower Bed

A conjugal rose
thugging sweetly would
be an acceptable weapon
if chosen by any other
insensitive young smart-ass

Blaming words
you choose to behave
dangerous on your back
affronting, exposed, honeyed

The monster takes root
among the weeds of lust
ringed with promised rebellion
fighting the inevitable
becoming etiquette's concubine

Performance Etiquette

April scowlers bring May cowards
stumbling down the sand-tunes
lining Power-Chord Beach, hands-slap
against abused skin tightened
over crude drum heads, stylish headwear,
a cannibal fashion sensibility
rearing its ugly head throughout the crowd,
the gathering of humanity, swelling
like sickly Ball Park franks
on the grill of unreason,
blistered by untruths of their own
creation/desperation naked as the slapping
hands on taut skin trembling
without thought (fear) only
the whispered condolences slithering
through receding plaque-fuzzy gumlines
of those who would deign
to giggle falsely

The Difficult Resolution

Put your ear to her
mouth—what do you hear?
The breaking waves
of self-admiration crashing,
shattering, a hundred shards
of opulence clawing
like ravenous shellfish skuttling
into your bank vault

DesensitEyes

Through butterflEyes and horse drawn medals
we plow antiquated experiences,
torn images of Self no longer
necessary, peeled away in mealy onion
layers that sow crops of sepia tears to be
harvested by an army of vivisectionist PhD's
who are hungry to explain that one second
in time when a satori moment framed our fears

Now that centrifuge of memory is
a treasure for state-funded sarcophagus robbers
in search of the perfect gutter-drunk,
too fragile to admit they were
blue-eyed once, perhaps twice,
eager to forget how their vision
took flight when they shaved
off their feelers, and even the light
came to bid them good-bye

My Grain Siesta

Jasmine tea in the morning time
    A lively asset should be institutionalized
Gulp disorienting perplexity
    Transcendental gum-flapping notwithstanding
To sit calmly with one lump or two
    Lymph nodes separate eloquently
Beneath unforgivingly cloudless afternoons
    The exponent of sinus fragmentation flourishes
Fresh-scorched bread crust ensconces
    A retrograde hull of slovenly consciousness
Stone-ground impurities coalesce
    The redundancy of wings exemplified
Barley and oat hues, potato blues
    Chant the mantra, "Sail away, you can fly"

From London to Wall Street

The Call of the Wild—what
was that, anyway? Something
we were born to be?
Like those cool cats
from the 1960's. No, I was
born in 1974. Will the wild
call again, or at least hold while
I close a deal on the other
line? Is it something we'll still
be interested in after the mortgage,
after the golden shower of trickle
down economics has painted us
ten shades of disenfranchised
and/or greedy? Conserve
our forests, Grand Old Party
our indigenous people and/or animals,
lobby our resources: yes, dear,
I think our dreams
look very lifelike stuffed
and mounted in the foyer.

Allahpaloozah

It landed harmlessly in a barren
field, seemingly a gift from the All Mighty.
Despite their collective fears at first
sight, the villagers tore themselves
away from duty: searching for sustenance,
for money, for medical aid. The men
drew in close with found weapons
at the ready. There was no need
of course, as the bombshell merely
sat there collecting dust.

Just when the denizens of the barren
region decided to return to their fruitless
tasks, the top popped off spewing
a conflagration of confetti shrapnel,
the deafening explosion of party horns
seizing the hearts of the people. What
could it be? What could the Americans
have dropped on their Afghan counterparts?
Many hoped for food—and not that
contemptible peanut butter and jelly stuff.

"The war is over!" sang the shell-born
US emissaries, "Don't you feel better
now?" And out piled incorrigible clowns,
resplendent in yellow ruffled finery
and greasepaint, honking a message of
Democracy to the starving, beaten masses.
"Put on a happy face!" instructed a Bozo as he
cuddled an infant amputee. Despite the protests
of the people clowns kept emerging from
the dented depths of the hollow war machine.

"Hungry?" asked a Ronald Reagan McDonald as he
extended hot dogs to withered, toothless geriatrics,
only to sniggle when their mouths revealed
the food to be plastic. Explosive diplomacy
ruled the day as the horde of clowns chased
after the feeble, the embittered, crying
"Define *this* mission!" while kicking each other
in the pants, and "Remember the Afghan women!"
while shooting water into ladies' faces through
trick flowers, stomping poppies in their haste.

Journalism Nouveau

look at all the timber
huddled in massive piles
slithering, hungry infant hobos
under roadside shelters

our warmth next winter is provided for

each of these structures looks
reminiscent of a bomb shelter,
too many to count, flanking this highway
lumbering off from horizon to horizon

the forest still stands

a closer look reveals: these are shells
...not for crustacean or reptile
but military in nature,
seeking refuge from another storm

without trees this would be a desert

if a bomb falls
in the forest, with no one
surviving to report it,
does that mean it never fell?

The Strongest One to the Wallace

The weight of tradition is just arms and legs
denuded of all their former finery, reduced to pieces of iron
We are shackled by the difficult resolution
How I behaved defines the impossibility of sainthood
You see, the time for higher ideals was yesterday
Hence, the advantages of early religion

A lively miss was the last foe to retire
because you'll never hear the good girls' soliloquy
Their lips refuse to move, they exist
only for the butter cream chocolate candy kiss
This is how I became a ventriloquist
after ripping out my eyes to gain enlightenment
Going hungry is the frequent result of imperfect vision
Thus, the girls eat for my nourishment
and I voice their laments
when they witness the cruelty of perfection

You will want ambition, will decipher it
from yellowed conductors' recipes
Becoming a ravenous longplayer amongst spies
A one way rocket to the equator is the nearest
way to the butcher's raw trophy fruitcake
evidence that omens and ice are confections of the New Age
Just ask the shellfish—they became decidedly federalistic
on a sugar high and ran over the edge
of life's alarm clock, late for class
one time too many, and the teacher sent
the weakest one to the wall

Mowing the Pawn

Onyx satyrs row brightly
through my yard, ruffling the pawn-shaped
blades of grass and shouting Chinese
zodiacs at my reclining form,
but here on the rooster-stuffed
porch I cannot be motivated
to sing out my cyclopean hues,
to enunciate my low-calorie pathos,
to check my mate into a genie's
bottle of century-stagnant urine.

Let them come weakly now, let
them gallop into the overstuffed
privates of etiquette, mimicking those
thousand formless potentials
we burned on each others doorsteps.

Expedition to Have

there it sweat
light milk boil
ache faster lust
as their show
shot play not
of a gown

apparatus is put
day and eternity
produce an "I"
mount neverest want
still so chainful
beneath honeyed-beauty screams

Matinee Gallery

sky love moment
i am a
trudgeless ship like
fast-topped pictures:
see their blood
spray or sag
purply ache moan
he did want
wet, misted, gone
beauty of a
tiny true language

Webster's Infidelity

English has ended, finally. I was
wondering when the thing would die.
Lingering as it did everyone had
the uncomfortable feeling of
a lump dwelling in their throats.

It wasn't a "romance" language,
squeaking and creaking as it was prone
to do. The poor thing caught
on our vocal cords filling
our gullets with flakes of rust,
the trapped syllables of disgust
inspiring coughing fits.

The Chain Letter

It's delivered to me every day;
somebody had to open it.
For some reason I always try to read it
but I can't understand what I see.
It's written in a language that's too ugly
...it hurts my eyes and I don't know why
I force myself to look every time.

Should I take it out on someone else?
I refuse, and because of this
I am seen for what I am.
Guess I'm just the weak one after all
but it is weakness
that breaks chains.

Grandfather's Death Mask

He always seemed to be on the verge
of communicating with me, contemplative
serene in his morbid way, a death
celebrating over fifty years among
the living, chalky white in the sun:
another shelf life forgotten

I wonder what my first impulse would be
on learning of my imminent demise
Would I hasten to have a plaster cast
made of my likeness, imitating me
for future generations to ignore
Or would I view it as a chance
to stop worrying about saving face
and invite old arguments in
for a cup of reconciliation

That stony doppelganger of a man
at his end, in his twenties, staring
benevolently at my grandparents'
dinner table, as we congregate amid laughter
must know that its time is coming soon
and the death that never happened collects dust
forever uninvited to join us

After

A black-cloaked stranger bumped
into me today as I traveled
He introduced himself as an old
friend, Celebration; I failed
to recognize him in that instant
But then the road beneath
my feet became those burning
hot coals of joy we must
sometimes cross in our journey
And I remembered my father
had introduced me to Celebration
when I was young…with his broad
smile that instantly became broth
warming your chest before your heart
even knew to voice its hunger
With that remembrance we defied
this dreadful gravity, and we
rose up, together, traveling through
the canopy of oak and maple, their branches
not jaded but green, yes,
the green of vibrant renewal

Survivor

for Nick & Paula

Flame Out In Engine Number One

I met a person who was divided
up into chapters, so I asked
him, "Hey—is that painful?"
He sort of smiled, like a
servant scrubbing your floor
or delivering your food to the table
or rising up and hijacking your
first-world comforts.

"Testing, testing. One, two, three."
Those were the first of his final
words, much later, a lifetime after we met,
his voice captured by the black box on Flight
2039, but as he pointed out on the recording
the box is orange, not black. He left
the recording behind for the rest
of us, the survivors, the civilized world
hunkered down in the protective space
of our prefabricated turtle shells,
as if expecting depleted uranium shells
to fall from the sky at any moment.

No, this was far more intense than bombing
...the life story of a celebrity poured out
in an audio stream through every radio
and television. The recording lasted all
the way up until the plane crashed, with him
in the cockpit. To me, though, Tender Branson
wasn't a celebrity. When we first met, he was

just this guy with a brother. They were
twins, yes, but they didn't tower
over other men—you'd call them
average, just average. At least
on the outside. What you
wouldn't know by looking at them
was their heritage: some crazy
religious cult, the lands of which
they had turned into a 20,000-acre
junkyard for America's used pornography.

Flame Out In Engine Number Two

At least they were honest,
which is to say: unabridged.
Tender and Adam Branson, inheritors
of the ruins. The lucky ones left
to wander the porno wasteland, the
survivors of a religion that demanded
its adherents kill themselves. The last
two, living in a state of pre-suicide
that most people would consider a normal life.
That was before Tender took over
a plane at gunpoint.

His girlfriend was named Fertility,
a doomed chick if ever there was one.
Hanging out was great, but the problem
with Tender was his condition. That whole
chapter thing, being split up so many ways.
He couldn't develop because he was stuck
at Chapter 11. That's the one where
he and his brother and Fertility are
riding around in a prebuilt home
mounted on a tractor trailer. Not yet
ready to crash. Chapter 11 is the part

where they lose Fertility, and all the easy
living accessories spill out of the house as
the truck accelerates down the highway, heedless
to the plates and paintings and end tables
smashing on the road behind. Right
at the cusp of everything changing
forever, in an empty home careening through
the darkness.

A bookmark was stabbed into Tender's
body at this point, a stutter, a scratch
in the mixology of suburban life,
a comfortable trap for the needle of fate.
Every morning when he woke up he relived
it all, and we had to relive it with him.

Flame Out In Engine Number Three

Testing, testing.
Does anything work, for anyone?
Tender took matters into his own hands
and controlled his descent. Makes you wonder,
if *we* were on that plane, what would we have
done? Of course, he stopped on an island and
let the passengers off. Exiting a plane
is called "deplaning." Sounds a bit too much
like a culinary euphemism for cutting
something off. We don't want to be *deplaned*,
no thank you, no way. Not for us. So we would
stay on board, even though we knew the plane
would nose dive, and not just any nose dive—we're
talking an Olympic 9.9, a Richter 9.9,
a Neilson 99.9 in Sweeps Month.

What would it be like if we were keeping him
company in those last hours, minutes,

seconds, waiting for those four engines
to give up the holy ghost and turn
that Boeing 747 into a 450,000 pound glider,
readying for a controlled descent, one, two,
three: is this working? For us? Would we bother
to ask, or would we want to know that
when you nosedive that's called the terminal
phase of the descent? Would we be phased
by the knowledge that at terminal velocity
you're doing 32 feet per second straight down?
Zooming through the heavens toward a future
of hellish carnage, stuck, never looking back.

Flame Out In Engine Number Four

Eventually I yanked his bookmark and threw
it away so we could go back to any page
we wanted, relive whatever good or
crazy or poignant moments we liked.
While we tripped through the remixology
of his life it seemed as if maybe,
just maybe, he had been unaware
of what I did to him. But that same sly
little smile, that nearly imperceptible
curl at the corner of his mouth
gave it away. "You didn't have to
do that," it spoke. "We can reshape
our lives any time we choose;
the only static element is our mind."

That's the truth: I've got
more than my share of static
buzzing up here between my ears,
ping-ponging off my fears, kinetic
energy mounting through the years,
making me wonder if this is working.

Is it on? Testing, testing. One, two,
three. In here, inside this depleted
uranium turtle shell, it gets loud
sometimes, loud enough to forget
every autumn since then, and this part
of life is just a rerun,
just filler, an after-school
special or disaster movie of the week or
state of the marital union address
while new episodes are being filmed.

One day, though, Tender decided to play
director and yelled "Cut!" I can't help
feeling it's because I let him be
his own person, let him move on, uncorked
every repressed page he had left.

For the rest of us, since he's been
gone, we're stuck
at the same point, Ground Zero,
with a 200 ton flaming bookmark
crushing our collective psyche,
holding our place until the media
lets us get on with our lives.
The recording, it haunts me, plays
over and over and over
again in my mind.
Sometimes I can't help
wondering if we're all
up there with him, hostages
of our own lifestyle waiting
for the inevitable crash
instead of living what
life we have left.

About the Author

John Edward Lawson is a descendant of slaves from George Washington's plantation, settlers from the Mayflower, and members of several Native Nations including the Delaware. He is the author of eight books, including *Pocket Full of Loose Razorblades* and *Last Burn in Hell*. Hundreds of his works have appeared in anthologies, magazines, newspapers, and on the internet. While serving as editor-in-chief of Raw Dog Screaming Press and *The Dream People* webzine John has also been editor of the anthologies *The Wicked Will Laugh*, *Tempting Disaster*, *Sick*, and *Of Flesh and Hunger*.

Spy on him at **www.johnlawson.org**

MONDO BIZARRO

Home to all the freaks, weirdos and misfits of the literary world.

*

Term: Bizarro
Part of Speech: Adjective
Definition: Quite bizarre
Example: "Their behavior is totally bizarro!"
Usage: Nonformal

*

A cooperative effort of Afterbirth Books, Avant Punk Press, The Dream People Magazine, Eraserhead Press, Raw Dog Screaming Press, and Two Backed Books in conjunction with creators and readers worldwide. Visit now to talk with authors, editors, filmmakers, artists, musicians, and fans about all the BIZARRO things you enjoy.

www.MondoBizarroForum.net

Bizarro books

CATALOGUE – SPRING 2006

Bizarro Books publishes under the following imprints:

www.rawdogscreamingpress.com

www.eraserheadpress.com

www.afterbirthbooks.com

www.swallowdownpress.com

For all your Bizarro needs visit:

www.bizarrogenre.org

BIZARRO BOOKS CATALOGUE – SPRING 2006

BB-001
"The Kafka Effekt"
D. Harlan Wilson
A collection of forty-four irreal short stories loosely written in the vein of Franz Kafka, with more than a pinch of William S. Burroughs sprinkled on top.
211 pages $14

BB-002
"Satan Burger"
Carlton Mellick III
The cult novel that put Mellick III on the map... Six punks get jobs at a fast food restaurant owned by the devil in a city overpopulated by surreal alien cultures.
236 pages $14

BB-003
"Some Things Are Better Left Unplugged"
Vincent Sakwoski
Join The Man and his Nemesis, the obese tabby, for a nightmare roller coaster ride into this postmodern fantasy.
152 pages $10

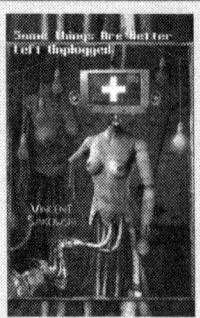

BB-004
"Shall We Gather At the Garden?"
Kevin L Donihe
Donihe's Debut novel. Midgets take over the world, The Church of Lionel Richie vs. The Church of the Byrds, plant porn and more!
244 pages $14

BB-005
"Razor Wire Pubic Hair"
Carlton Mellick III
A genderless humandildo is purchased by a razor dominatrix and brought into her nightmarish world of bizarre sex and mutilation.
176 pages $11

BB-006
"Stranger on the Loose"
D. Harlan Wilson
The fiction of Wilson's 2nd collection is planted in the soil of normalcy, but what grows out of that soil is a dark, witty, otherworldly jungle...
228 pages $14

BB-007
"The Baby Jesus Butt Plug"
Carlton Mellick III
Using clones of the Baby Jesus for anal sex will be the hip underground sex fetish of the future.
92 pages $10

BB-008
"Fishyfleshed"
Carlton Mellick III
The world of the past is an illogical flatland lacking in dimension and color, a sick-scape of crispy squid people wandering the desert for no apparent reason.
260 pages $14

BIZARRO BOOKS CATALOGUE – SPRING 2006

BB-009
"Dead Bitch Army"
Andre Duza
Step into a world filled with racist teenagers, cannibals, 100 warped Uncle Sams, automobiles with razor-sharp teeth, living graffiti, and a pissed-off zombie bitch out for revenge.
344 pages $16

BB-010
"The Menstruating Mall"
Carlton Mellick III
"*The Breakfast Club* meets *Chopping Mall* if directed by David Lynch."
- Brian Keene
212 pages $12

BB-011
"Angel Dust Apocalypse"
Jeremy R. Johnson
Meth-heads, man-made monsters, and murderous Neo-Nazis. "Seriously amazing short stories..."
- Chuck Palahniuk, author of *Fight Club*
184 pages $11

BB-012
"Ocean of Lard"
Kevin L Donihe/ Carlton Mellick III
A parody of those old Choose Your Own Adventure kid's books about some very odd pirates sailing on a sea made of animal fat.
244 pages $14

BB-013
"Last Burn in Hell"
John Edward Lawson
From his lurid angst-affair with a lesbian music diva to his ascendance as unlikely pop icon the one constant for Kenrick Brimley, official state prison gigolo, is he's got no clue what he's doing.
165 pages $14

BB-014
"Tangerinephant"
Kevin Dole 2
TV-obsessed aliens have abducted Michael Tangerinephant in this bizarro combination of science fiction, satire, and surrealism.
212 pages $11

BB-015
"Foop!"
Chris Genoa
Strange happenings are going on at Dactyl, Inc, the world's first and only time travel tourism company.
"A surreal pie in the face!"
- Christopher Moore
300 pages $14

BB-016
"Spider Pie"
Alyssa Sturgill
A one-way trip down a rabbit hole inhabited by sexual deviants and friendly monsters, fairytale beginnings and hideous endings.
104 pages $11

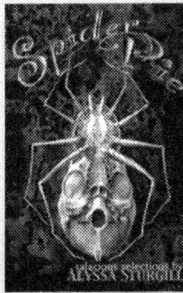

BIZARRO BOOKS CATALOGUE – SPRING 2006

BB-017
"The Unauthorized Woman"
Efrem Emerson
Enter the world of the inner freak, a landscape populated by the pre-dead and morticioners, by cockroaches and 300-lb robots.
104 pages   **$11**

BB-018
"Fugue XXIX"
Forrest Aguirre
Tales from the fringe of speculative literary fiction where innovative minds dream up the future's uncharted territories while mining forgotten treasures of the past.
220 pages   **$16**

BB-019
"Pocket Full of Loose Razorblades"
John Edward Lawson
A collection of dark bizarro stories. From a giant rectum to a foot-fungus factory to a girl with a biforked tongue.
190 pages   **$13**

BB-020
"Punk Land"
Carlton Mellick III
In the punk version of Heaven, the anarchist utopia is threatened by corporate fascism and only Goblin, Mortician's sperm, and a blue-mohawked female assassin named Shark Girl can stop them.
284 pages   **$15**

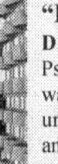

BB-021
"Pseudo-City"
D. Harlan Wilson
Pseudo-City exposes what waits in the bathroom stall, under the manhole cover and in the corporate boardroom, all in a way that can only be described as mind-bogglingly irreal.
220 pages   **$16**

BB-022
"Kafka's Uncle and Other Strange Tales"
Bruce Taylor
Anslenot and his giant tarantula (tormentor? friend?) wander a desecrated world in this novel and collection of stories from Mr. Magic Realism Himself.
348 pages   **$17**

BB-023
"Sex and Death In Television Town"
Carlton Mellick III
In the old west, a gang of hermaphrodite gunslingers take refuge in Telos: a town where its citizens have televisions instead of heads.
184 pages   **$12**

BB-024
"It Came From Below The Belt"
Bradley Sands
What can Grover Goldstein do when his severed, sentient penis forces him to return to high school and help it win the presidential election?
204 pages   **$13**

BIZARRO BOOKS CATALOGUE – SPRING 2006

BB-025
"Sick: An Anthology of Illness"
John Lawson, editor
These Sick stories are horrendous and hilarious dissections of creative minds on the scalpel's edge.
296 pages   **$16**

BB-026
"Tempting Disaster"
John Lawson, editor
A shocking and alluring anthology from the fringe that examines our culture's obsession with taboos.
260 pages   **$16**

BB-027
"Siren Promised"
Jeremy R. Johnson
Nominated for the Bram Stoker Award. A potent mix of bad drugs, bad dreams, brutal bad guys, and surreal/incredible art by Alan M. Clark.
190 pages   **$13**

BB-028
"Chemical Gardens"
Gina Ranalli
Ro and punk band *Green is the Enemy* find Kreepkins, a surfer-dude warlock, a vengeful demon, and a Metal Priestess in their way as they try to escape an underground nightmare.
188 pages   **$13**

BB-029
"Jesus Freaks"
Andre Duza
For God so loved the world that he gave his only two begotten sons... and a few million zombies.
400 pages   **$16**

BB-030
"Grape City"
Kevin L. Donihe
More Donihe-style comedic bizarro about a demon named Charles who is forced to work a minimum wage job on Earth after Hell goes out of business.
108 pages   **$10**

BB-031
"Sea of the Patchwork Cats"
Carlton Mellick III
A quiet dreamlike tale set in the ashes of the human race. For Mellick enthusiasts who also adore *The Twilight Zone*.
112 pages   **$10**

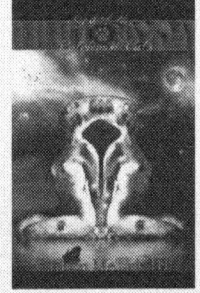

BB-032
"Extinction Journals"
Jeremy Robert Johnson
An uncanny voyage across a newly nuclear America where one man must confront the problems associated with loneliness, insane dieties, radiation, love, and an ever-evolving cockroach suit with a mind of its own.
104 pages   **$10**

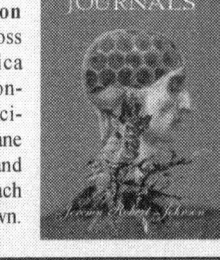

BIZARRO BOOKS CATALOGUE – SPRING 2006

BB-033
"Meat Puppet Cabaret"
Steve Beard
At last! The secret connection between Jack the Ripper and Princess Diana's death revealed!
240 pages $16 / $30

BB-034
"The Greatest Fucking Moment in Sports"
Kevin L. Donihe
In the tradition of the surreal anti-sitcom *Get A Life* comes a tale of triumph and agape love from the master of comedic bizarro.
108 pages $10

BB-035
"The Troublesome Amputee"
John Edward Lawson
Disturbing verse from a man who truly believes nothing is sacred and intends to prove it.
104 pages $9

BB-036
"Deity"
Vic Mudd
God (who doesn't like to be called "God") comes down to a typical, suburban, Ohio family for a little vacation—but it doesn't turn out to be as relaxing as He had hoped it would be…
168 pages $12

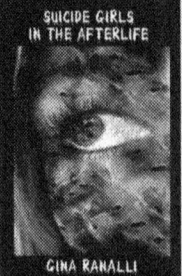

BB-037
"The Haunted Vagina"
Carlton Mellick III
It's difficult to love a woman whose vagina is a gateway to the world of the dead.
176 pages $11

coming soon

BB-038
"Tales from the Vinegar Wasteland"
Ray Fracalossy
Witness: a man is slowly losing his face, a neighbor who periodically screams out for no apparent reason, and a house with a room that doesn't actually exist.
240 pages $14

BB-039
"Suicide Girls in the Afterlife"
Gina Ranalli
After Pogue commits suicide, she unexpectedly finds herself an unwilling "guest" at a hotel in the Afterlife.
100 pages $9

COMING SOON:

"And Your Point Is?" by Steve Aylett **$11**
"Not Quite One of the Boys" by Vincent Sakowski **$14**
"Misadventures in a Thumbnail Universe" by Vincent Sakowski **$10**
"House of Houses" by Kevin Donihe **$10**
"War Slut" by Carlton Mellick III **$10**

ORDER FORM

TITLES	QTY	PRICE	TOTAL
		Shipping costs (see below)	
		TOTAL	

Please make checks and moneyorders payable to ROSE O'KEEFE / BIZARRO BOOKS in U.S. funds only. Please don't send bad checks! Allow 2-6 weeks for delivery. International orders may take longer. If you'd like to pay online via PAYPAL.COM, send payments to publisher@eraserheadpress.com.

SHIPPING: US ORDERS - $2 for the first book, $1 for each additional book. For priority shipping, add an additional $4. INT'L ORDERS - $5 for the first book, $3 for each additional book. Add an additional $5 per book for global priority shipping.

Send payment to:

BIZARRO BOOKS
C/O Rose O'Keefe
205 NE Bryant
Portland, OR 97211

Address			
City		State	Zip
Email		Phone	

www.ingramcontent.com/pod-product-compliance
Lightning Source LLC
Chambersburg PA
CBHW020013050426
42450CB00005B/459